EFFECTIVE COMMUNICATION FOR THE ACCOUNTANT

Trevor J Bentley

KOGAN PAGE

Published by Kogan Page Ltd
in association with
the Chartered Institute of Management Accountants
|C| I |m|A|
Incorporated by Royal Charter
63 Portland Place
London W1N 4AB

Throughout this book reference to the male gender implies also the female gender.

First published in 1988 by
Kogan Page Ltd,
120 Pentonville Rd, London N1 9JN
in association with the Chartered Institute of Management Accountants, 63 Portland Place, London W1N 4AB.

Printed in Great Britain by
Billing & Sons Ltd, Worcester

British Library Cataloguing in Publication Data

Bentley, Trevor J.
    Effective communication for the accountant.
    1. Accounting. Communication
    I. Title
    657'.0141

ISBN 1 85091 520 2

Contents

		Page
Preface		9
1. Introduction		11
2. Communication Principles		15
	Purpose	16
	Formation	17
	Transmission	18
	Reception	19
	Perception	19
	Action	20
	Barriers to Communication	21
3. Signals and Messages		23
	Words	24
	Numbers	25
	Symbols	26
	Pictures	27
	Gestures	27
	Sounds	29
4. The Written Word		31
	The Reader	32
	Asking Questions	34
	Writing a Letter	35
	Writing Instructions	36
	Technical Literature	38
	Report Writing	39

5. The Spoken Word   45
  Meetings   48
  Using the Telephone   53
  Presentation Techniques   55

6. Visual Media   61
  Pictures   62
  Cartoons and Illustrations   62
  Diagrams   62
  Charts and Graphs   62
  Signs   68

7. Barriers to Communication   69
  Language   69
  Vocabulary   69
  Class   70
  Attitude   70
  Position   70
  Personality and Character   71
  Mood   71
  Knowledge of Subject   71
  The Transmitter   72
  Communication Needs   73

8. Effective Communication   75

Index   77

List of Figures

Fig. 3.1 The presentation of figures in tables   26
Fig. 3.2 Deceiving the brain   28
Fig. 3.3 The use of pictures as a means of communication   28
Fig. 4.1 A typical business letter layout   37
Fig. 6.1 Information represented in the form of a table   63
Fig. 6.2 Information represented in the form of a graph   64
Fig. 6.3 Information represented in the form of a bar chart   65
Fig. 6.4 Information represented in the form of a block chart   66
Fig. 6.5 Information represented in the form of a progress   67
          chart

Preface

This book is about communication and communicators. It is about how every individual can improve their communication skills. It is aimed specifically at accountants, not because they have a greater need, many are excellent communicators, but because effective communication is such an important and fundamental part of the accountant's job.

As an accountant I have been fortunate in the positions I have held, in the people I have worked with and in the training I have received. This book is a test of my communication skills as is everything I write or say. If you fail to grasp my message then I have failed as a communicator. You can never blame the recipient of your message if he misunderstands it.

To communicate effectively you must think of your audience. You must then structure your message and your method of delivery to be most easily received and understood. This book emphasises the approach of putting the audience first. In addition, there are many simple ideas on how you can become a more effective communicator.

Chapter One

Introduction

The accountant is called upon to communicate in a wide variety of situations. He has to talk to people, attend meetings, carry out interviews, prepare reports, address meetings and conferences, prepare financial statements both internal and external, and both make and receive telephone calls in a variety of situations. All of these activities provide an opportunity for effective or ineffective communication to take place. Though these situations will differ and seem to present the accountant with a never-ending challenge, there are really only 14 different situations:

- *Ad hoc* face to face discussion
- Telephone calls — making
                              receiving
- Corresponding
- Meetings — attending
                      chairing
- Report writing — informative
                              discussive
                              persuasive
                              explanatory
- Financial statements
- Presentations — informal
                              formal
- Interviews.

The advice given in this book will help in all 14 situations, creating communication opportunities and overcoming communication problems.

The accountant is unique in the business world for the depth and scope of the subject matter he has to deal with. He is involved at all levels of the business collecting and processing data, and disseminating information. Virtually all business activities have a financial implication which will be analysed and understood by the decision-makers responsible for the activities. This places a burden on the accountant not only in analysing the implications but in communicating them effectively so that they are fully understood by everyone.

The accountant is almost permanently employed in the process of communication. If the accountant allocates his or her time to the 14 situations listed above I doubt if there would be much time left over for financial analysis. Yet, despite this emphasis on communication activities, many accountants would not describe themselves as communicators. Why should this be the case? I believe that there are four reasons why the accountant does not see his primary role as a communicator.

The first of these is associated with the normal education and training process undertaken by accountants. The emphasis is on analysis procedures, methods, rules, mechanics and the implications of financial and economic factors for business. The fact that most accountants can speak and write coherently is judged sufficient to enable them to be effective communicators.

The second main reason is the language of accounting. Like all technical languages, accounting jargon is useful as a shorthand way for people who are members of the accounting family to communicate. For people outside the family circle the accounting language is a distinct barrier inhibiting communication as the accountant practises it.

The third reason that the accountant fails to recognise his role as a communicator is because his colleagues regard him as a poor one. They often hold up what he says and what he writes as an example of poor communication.

The final reason is, I believe, the accountant's unwillingness to display his lack of ability as an effective communicator. To claim you are a communicator when you lack the knowledge and skills to carry out the role effectively, is tantamount to managerial suicide.

To overcome these problems requires knowledge and skill in effective communication and the willingness and desire to practise at an early opportunity. To be able to speak and write in the language of the audience is the first essential ingredient. The good communicator must learn how to use the language both spoken and written to achieve the desired result.

There are many ways in which messages can be constructed and delivered. The good communicator is able to select the most appropriate way for the purpose he wants to achieve.

The accountant relies mainly on numbers. The vast majority of written material produced by accountants is numerical. Numbers are powerful when used effectively, but not for every occasion. The accountant's approach is to produce numbers interspersed with words, whereas most other people use words interspersed with numbers.

The first step, then, is for the accountant to recognise the importance of his role as a communicator.

The second is to develop his knowledge and skill in the effective use of the language of his audience.

The third step is to learn how to utilise the wide range of communications media to deliver his message effectively.

And finally, the accountant must develop an awareness of his communication ability by recognising and accepting that any failure of his audience to understand is due to his own failure to communicate effectively.

Chapter Two

Communication Principles

There is only one objective in communication and that is to pass a signal (or message) to an individual or group of individuals that is understood and responded to in the way desired by the communicator.

The means of achieving this desired result is known as the communication process and consists of the following stages:

- Purpose — what is the communicator trying to achieve
- Formation — construction of the message in the most suitable form
- Transmission — selection of the most appropriate means of transferring the message from the communicator to his audience
- Reception — consideration of how the message will be received
- Perception — determining the way the message will be interpreted
- Action — deciding how to trigger the appropriate response and how to receive feedback on the response produced.

Purpose

There are a variety of purposes for which the accountant will use communication —

- To inform
- To explain
- To instruct
- To advise
- To persuade
- To sell
- To discuss
- To question.

In each instance the purpose and the context in which the communication will take place will affect the accountant's choice of action.

All communication is a two-party process: it is the process of transferring knowledge effectively between two individuals or groups. It requires firstly a communicator and secondly a receiver. The communicator will create the message (knowledge) and transmit it to the receiver. The receiver will then interpret the message and, it is hoped, act accordingly.

It is important that the communicator ('transmitter') decides the response he wants to obtain from the receiver before he starts the communication process. This is the purpose that he wants to achieve:

- To inform so that the receiver is fully aware
- To explain so that the receiver completely understands
- To instruct so that the receiver learns the correct techniques
- To advise so that the receiver takes appropriate action

- To persuade so that the receiver acts in agreement
- To sell so that the receiver 'buys' and is not conscious of being 'sold'
- To discuss so that the receiver agrees the basis of opinion or comment
- To question so that the receiver provides relevant answers.

It is the achievement of the desired attitude and behaviour of the receiver which determines the success of the communication. It does not matter how much time and effort goes into the construction of the message and the transmission; if the receiver does not respond as expected, the communicator has failed.

The communicator must therefore ask and answer the following questions before proceeding:

- Who am I communicating with?
- How do I want this person or these people to respond?
- What do I want them to do on receiving my communication?
- What do I want them to know on receiving my communication?

It is the responsibility of the transmitter to ensure that the purpose is clear and that the communication process is carried through successfully.

Formation

Construction of the message in the most suitable form is impossible if the purpose is not absolutely clear. The message must be constructed so that the receiver interprets it in the way it is intended. It is much easier to tell someone he is to receive a pay rise than to tell him he is redundant. Good news is easier to transmit and more readily received than bad news. But the way the message is conducted is not the only factor.

The reason for the communication obviously affects the content of the message and its structure. It might be a simple directive where one word will suffice, such as instructing a gun crew to 'fire', or a complex, lengthy explanation of the implications of inflation on annual accounts.

The choice of how to construct the message will depend upon the transmitter's interpretation of the receiver's 'wave length'. The way the receiver will best be able to receive and interpret the information contained in the message is fundamental to the way it is constructed. Messages usually consist of a mixture of the following:

- Words
- Numbers
- Symbols
- Pictures
- Gestures.

These must be used with care so that the message is clear and unambiguous when it is received.

Transmission

The transmission process involves choosing the most appropriate way to get the message from the mind of the transmitter into the mind of the receiver, both of whom interpret the message in the same way. There are many ways in which this can be done (see Chapter Four).

The choice will depend upon the circumstances and will not always enable the transmitter to choose his ideal approach. This immediately creates a barrier to successful communication.

The choice of the most appropriate method will depend upon such factors as time, distance, impact as well as the purpose, the circumstances, the mechanics available and, of course, the transmitter and receiver themselves.

Reception

For communication to work the receiver must 'get the message', understand the message, interpret its meaning correctly and act accordingly. For this to happen not only must the message be constructed properly and delivered in the best possible way, it must also arrive at a time, place and in conditions such that the receiver is willing and prepared to receive it.

The transmitter will succeed in getting his message across if he makes sure, as far as possible, that his message arrives at an appropriate occasion. This is much easier to state than it is to do, but a little bit of effort in trying to make it happen is usually well worthwhile. It might only take a moment to check when the receiver will be available to receive your message and to warn him of its arrival. But even this simple approach can make an enormous difference.

Perception

Perception is the process of receiving, recognising and interpreting signals so as to gain awareness of their meaning and implications. It is obvious that this must take place in the mind of the receiver before any communication can take place.

There are three key words in the first part of this definition; receiving, recognising and interpreting. Firstly, the message must reach the mind of the receiver and his senses—sight, hearing, taste, touch and smell. Secondly, the signals received must be recognised, ie they must be known and identifiable. Thirdly, the signals must be capable of being interpreted, ie they must be linked in such a way that the persons mind can derive a meaning from them.

The brain receives visual images and sounds and checks them against a library of images and sounds previously developed from education, training and experience. If there is an exact or similar image or sound on file the brain checks the meaning or meanings already stored and relates them to the circumstances. If there is a match or near match the brain assigns an interpretation to the signals and if necessary acts accordingly.

The transmitter can help this process to work by using images and sounds (words) which are likely to be in the receivers mental library and have the desired meaning already attached to them. In this way, the brain will be able to create a suitable match and apply an appropriate meaning.

Once the meaning has been derived the implications for the receiver can be determined and the appropriate response generated.

Action

The final part of the communication process is for the receiver to respond in the desired way. This may be a very direct, simple action or a more complex series of actions.

The response to the directive 'fire' would be the pressing of a button to activate the firing mechanism. The communication process can be seen quite clearly in this example.

Purpose   — to get the gunner to fire the gun
Formation   — the word 'fire'

Transmission — word 'fire' is shouted within the hearing of the gunner

Reception   — the gunner hears the word 'fire'

Perception   — the word 'fire' is recognised, and means in this context press the firing mechanism

Action   — the gunner presses the firing mechanism.

Barriers to Communication

This process, so simply described in the above example, has to overcome many barriers, most of which are created by the people involved. The main problems to be faced are dealt with fully in Chapter Seven. For the moment we will record the fact that good communicators recognise that barriers exist and take the responsibility for overcoming them.

If they are transmitters then they take pains to make it as easy as possible for the receiver to 'get the message'. If they are receivers they make it as easy as possible for the transmitter to 'get the message across'. The role of the accountant as a communicator can be described by the following well-known saying—they must be able to

'explain to those who can't understand, and
understand those who can't explain.'

Chapter Three

Signals and Messages

Human beings have always used their senses to receive signals to warn of danger. The principal senses are those of sight and sound, which allow signals to be transmitted over long distances. For signals to be effective as a method of communication they must be easily recognised and interpreted. Signals warning of danger must be sufficiently obvious to draw the receiver's individual attention to them. Bright colours and loud noises are examples of simple and effective signals.

By linking signals together in sequence, complex messages can be transmitted. Native drums and smoke signals are early examples of using sequences of signals in this way. Later, flags and Morse code were used.

Modern communication is still based on the concept of signals directed at the human senses, but these signals now take many different forms, including:

- Words
- Numbers
- Symbols
- Pictures
- Gestures
- Sounds.

When arranged in appropriate sequences these signals provide the basis for messages from the very simple warning sirens to complex multi-media presentations, reinforcing subtle messages.

One of the primary skills in communication is that of being able to arrange signals in the most effective way to make the resultant message intelligible to the receiver.

Words

Words are the basic elements of language. When linked together in a prescribed way they provide a means of describing, explaining and expressing an unlimited range of emotions, feelings, expressions, etc. Sentences are held together within the language by the rules that exist within its grammar.

Grammar is a systematic description of the way a language works. It describes the individual words that occur in a language, the forms they take and the ways speakers and writers put them together in meaningful combinations.

Individual words have a certain meaning which is held in the brain alongside the library of sounds, that are recognised as that particular word. Let us take two words in order to see how this works. Consider the words BLUE and SKY. Each has a particular meaning in the mind. When we link words together the meaning is adapted depending on the order of the words we use. BLUE SKY means something different from SKY BLUE.

As we increase the number of words in the combination, so we can extend and adapt our meaning. If we also consider the inflexion we put on words then the scope is enormous, for example:

LANCASHIRE ARE PLAYING CRICKET

has quite a different meaning from

ARE LANCASHIRE PLAYING CRICKET?

To use words effectively it is necessary to know how to put words together in simple, easy-to-understand combinations. The basic combination of words is the sentence, which should be simple, short and have unity of thought.

Sentences are usually grouped in paragraphs which have a common theme. These basic rules are true whether words are used in speaking or writing. The key to using words in communication is to concentrate on simple words in simple combinations, emphasising clarity and brevity.

Numbers

Numbers are special symbols for words that describe quantities. They are a form of shorthand which makes the manipulation of quantities easier. They are used in conjunction with words or on their own. It is normal for numbers to be presented either in columns or rows, or in the form of mathematical notation.

Numbers are the accountant's primary combination symbol, and the most usual combination is the columns and rows approach. Such communication is nearly always in writing as it is very difficult to communicate numbers and their relationship in the spoken word.

There are three golden rules for communicating using numbers. These are concerned with

a) significance
b) order
c) layout.

Significance — remove the insignificant many and concentrate on the significant few.

As a general guide, aim to have no more than four figures across the column. In Figure 3.1 the significance would be determined largely by the variance column. If the figures had been expressed in millions the significance of the variances would have been lost.

Order — numbers should be presented in the order which matches the receiver's interest rather than in strict logical order.

It is normal, as in Figure 3.1, for the most interesting numbers to

	ACTUAL	BUDGET	VARIANCE		ACTUAL	BUDGET	VARIANCE
	£	£	£		£ 000	£ 000	£ 000
Sales	7,385,219	8,000,000	(614,781)	Sales	7,385	8,000	(615)
Direct Costs:				Direct Costs:			
Labour	1,765,820	1,800,000	34,180	Labour	1,766	1,800	34
Materials	2,451,875	2,500,000	48,125	Materials	2,452	2,500	48
Manufacture	1,811,911	2,000,000	188,089	Manufacture	1,812	2,000	188
	6,029,606	6,300,000	270,394		6,030	6,300	270
Contribution	1,355,613	1,700,000	(344,387)	Contribution	1,355	1,700	(345)
		WRONG				RIGHT	

Figure 3.1   The presentation of figures in tables

appear at the bottom right hand corner of many accounting reports. This is because convention and mathematical logic dictates this approach. The approach can be improved by preceding the table with a sentence such as:

'In the following table there is an adverse contribution variance of £345,000 which is 20% of the budget. This is due to a lower level of sales (£615,000 less than budget), only partially offset by favourable direct and cost variances of £270,000.'

This sentence directs attention at the most important numbers and guides the reader's examination of the figures.

Layout — use space and dividing lines to punctuate numbers so that the eye can make sense of them.

Symbols

Symbols are used primarily in written and visual communications. They cover such items as punctuation, mathematical notation, musical notation, signs, etc. They overcome the problems of different languages and are more easily learned than the relevant words.

They can be extremely effective when used imaginatively for communication of information, particularly when used in conjunction with graphical presentation. Symbols enable fast meaningful recognition to take place, as long as the brain of the receiver can recognise, if not fully then substantially, the symbols presented.

Symbols can also replace groups of words with simple visual signals, as in these few examples:

In Words	Symbolically
Three (is less than) five	$3 < 5$
This (is equal to) that	this $=$ that
X (is less than or equal to) Y	$X \leqslant Y$

Pictures

According to the Chinese proverb

'A picture is worth a thousand words'.

But this is true only if the picture describes what is wanted and if the receiver is able to give the desired meaning to the visual message. The eye (when it works properly) is a very accurate receiver of images. However it is still necessary for the brain to check its files and ascribe a meaning to the visual signals received. The brain can be tricked. Optical illusions, such as that shown in Figure 3.2, can confuse the brain. The brain imposes its own (in this case, erroneous) interpretation on what turns out to be a confused visual image.

Visual images can have a powerful impact and can be much better than words for communicating particular messages. Figure 3.3 shows a picture of a house being renovated. The picture tells a clear story, and is a concise visual progress report.

Gestures

Signals can be given simply by the way people move and use their hands and faces. This is referred to as body language and is usually very meaningful, once a person has learned how to interpret the signals. Frowns, raised eyebrows, a smile, a shrug of the shoulders, nervous tapping of the figures, the slight nod or shake of the head, all

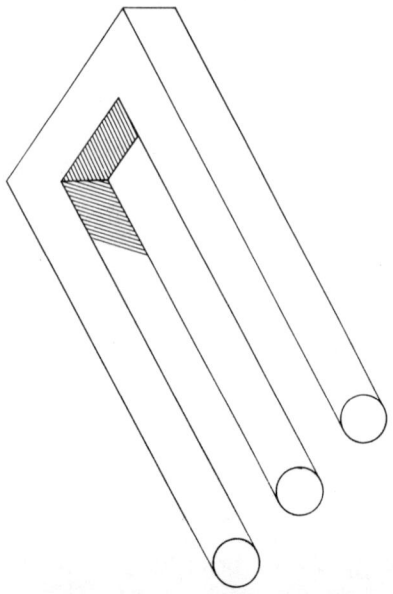

Figure 3.2   Deceiving the brain

Figure 3.3   The use of pictures as a means of communiction

convey a particular meaning within the context of what is happening at the time the gesture is made.

The use of hands can become a language in itself, for example the sign language used by the deaf and the language used on the racecourse by the tic-tac men. The use of gestures must not be underestimated as a means of communication. When linked with the spoken word, gestures can change the whole meaning of what is being said.

Sounds

Words when spoken are sounds that we have come to receive and understand in a certain way. Different languages are learned through the process of learning to recognise sounds and associate a meaning to them. When we first learn to read we do so by converting the symbols we see into sounds which we recognise through association with visual images presented at the same time.

Gradually we associate the symbols directly to the visual images, without having to make the sounds. However, many people still follow the same procedure in the brain: they see the symbol, they associate it with a sound, and they then give the sound a meaning.

Sounds and visual images are the primary records within the brain that we use for communication. However, the association of the other senses of touch, taste and smell with sounds and images provides us with a very sophisticated repertoire of devices to promote effective communication.

Chapter Four

The Written Word

The accountant is almost certainly involved in some form of written communication every working day. There are numerous ways in which the written word is used as a means of communication. The main ones which are examined in this book are:

- Correspondence and written instructions
- Technical literature
- Reports.

These three forms of written communication are the principal ones used by the accountant. They require the writer to follow the basic rules of written communications which are concerned with

a) The audience
b) The subject
c) The writer's objectives.

The audience
The writer must give careful thought to the intended reader, and prepare his material to obtain the reaction he wants from the reader. The audience for any piece of writing could cover a wide range of experience, background and position. This is particularly true of technical papers and reports but less so for correspondence. Careful understanding of the readership and their interests is essential to successful written communication.

The subject
The way words are used can depend upon the subject being communicated. If the subject concerns something pleasant then the

words used will be light and easy, even humorous; if the context concerns something unpleasant then the words must be simple and direct with no emotional inflexion. The possible reactions of the audience to the subject must also be considered, so that the best mix of words can be selected.

The objectives
Every piece of written material should have quite clear cut objectives. These can fall into a number of categories, the main ones are:

- What should the reader know
- What should the reader understand
- How should the reader react
- What should the reader do.

Of course not all communication seeks to achieve all these objectives. Whatever is trying to be achieved should be carefully considered before the writing starts.

The Reader
The reader is the only person who matters and before writing we must ask ourselves, 'Do I know my reader?' If the reader can be positively identifed, then do so. The composition of the subject contained in correspondence can be affected by a knowledge of their receiver.

There are some barriers to written communication which we can control. These are:

- The language used
- The vocabulary
- Our profession
- Our position
- The knowledge of the subject we are writing about.

But we only have a limited control over the following attributes of our receivers:

- Attitude
- Mood
- Personality
- Character.

We have absolutely no control over the conditions in which our written communication is to be read. Therefore it is important that we keep our written work:

- Simple
- Clear
- Sincere
- Brief.

Simplicity enables ease of reading, which promotes interpretation, and good interpretation gives the right foundation for understanding. Simple writing means the avoidance of:

- The mingling of unnecessary words, excessive ornaments, useless frills
- Too much formality
- Annoying ostentation (putting on an appearance).

However, simplicity must not remove or cloud sincerity.

Sincerity in writing is a great gift as it can prevent writing from being misunderstood and removes the possibility of the writer being misrepresented in the reader's mind. Sincerity is also the enemy of hypocrisy and deceit. Furthermore, it confirms purpose and conveys to the reader a shared self-confidence, an aura of well-being and usefulness.

If the aim of writing is to persuade someone of something, then it is necessary to be sincere—the slightest tinge of insincerity will almost certainly be detected by the reader.

Clarity is all important when writing as it assists in the understanding of the subject. It removes the need for subjective questioning by the reader, and therefore assists the writer in guiding the reader to his goal.

Being brief saves other people's time and money. Bernard Shaw once ended a letter with the comment, 'I am sorry to write such a long letter, I didn't have the time to write a shorter one.' Do not be too brief, however, since the reader may incorrectly assume that the writer is being either curt (ie discourteously brief) or abrupt (ie disconnected). Once someone has formed such an impression, it is very difficult to change it.

Asking Questions

Asking questions and finding answers is an essential part of communicating. The need to ask questions usually arises from two situations. The first is the need for more knowledge, the second comes from the need for clarification.

When constructing questions, the question must not become a challenge to the reader or make them feel they are being interrogated.

When answering questions, be sure to read the question properly and make sure that it is understood. Then answer the question in simple direct terms, giving the reader the information required.

If it is necessary to answer or write a letter of complaint, then it is essential to avoid rudeness. There is no excuse for rudeness; complaints can be lodged unemotionally. Sarcasm—the lowest form of wit—should also be avoided. Threatening letters are even worse. They usually only annoy people and they rarely achieve satisfaction.

The golden rule of complaint writing and complaint answering is to be excruciatingly polite. Make your point clearly, firmly and be explicit.

When replying to a complaint avoid being evasive and patronis-
ing. This can make the writer look ridiculous in the eyes of the
reader, who will think that the writer is trying to excuse himself. If the
writer is in the wrong, then he should say so. If someone else has
failed in the organisation, reprimand them, but assert the blame
courteously and inform the offended party of the steps being taken
to put the complaint right. An aggressive reply has an irritating,
negative effect and only results in the complainant digging his
heels in.

So, when specifically answering a complaint, be apologetic about
what has happened and firm about the action to be taken, and leave
it at that.

Apply the rules of sincerity to maintain goodwill.

Always respond immediately with an informed reply. The worst
reply that can be given is the old chestnut, 'Your complaint is being
investigated and we will keep you informed'. This not only loses any
goodwill that existed, it also promotes anger and frustration in the
complainant.

Writing a Letter

Before writing any letter, the proposed contents must be analysed
and defined. The purpose of the letter should be summed up in its
objective, only then is a letter ready to be written.

There is no one correct way to write a letter so we will examine a
layout which can reliably be used for a great many purposes.

The letter should start by identifying who is writing to whom. On
standard letterheads it is normal for the name of the company to
appear at the top, and for memos to be headed 'from' and 'to'. The
second item on a letter is the name and address of the intended
reader. The subject of the letter should then be stated.

The body of the letter should be written in three sections. The introduction sets out briefly the reason for the letter. The second section deals with the points the writer wants to make, including any questions, answers, etc. The final section presents a brief summary and ends with a statement of the action requested on the reader's next steps.

The final salutation should be appropriate to the level of formality. The use of the PS is very effective if it is used to make an important additional point. Some experienced writers use the PS to make the main point of the letter but it is easy to overwork this device.

An example of the layout we suggest is shown in Figure 4.1.

Writing Instructions

When a letter or memo is used to give instructions it becomes a special kind of communication. Written instructions should contain four elements:

a) The reason for the instructions
b) The specific instructions themselves
c) The date when they should come into effect
d) The person who is to take responsibility for carrying out the instructions.

There must be no ambiguity and the writer must make very sure that the readers cannot misunderstand.

Instructions must be written in very clear, directional language. Words such as 'must', 'will' and 'shall' should be used, and the salutations should be short and precise. It is also a good idea to send everyone two copies and ask them to sign and return one copy indicating that they have understood the instructions and will act accordingly.

CNJ Systems Ltd

102 Station Parade, Harrogate, North Yorkshire, HG1 1HQ.
Tel: Harrogate (0423) 522461

Mr. George Staples,
Springfield,
Taylor Lane,
Barwick-in-Elmet,
Leeds.

15th September 1987

Dear George,

I am writing on behalf of myself and my colleagues to say
thank you for your contribution to our Selling Skills
Course last week at the Belsfield.

We have all agreed that the course was most successful, due
in much part to your invaluable contribution. I am well aware
of the amount of effort you put into your role as George
Sugar, and I am pleased to say that my colleagues enjoyed
both your performance and your company.

Please find enclosed a token of our appreciation for the
time you gave up to help us.

Once again thank you very much indeed for helping.

Best wishes.

Yours sincerely,

DR TREVOR J. BENTLEY
Managing Director

ENC.

TJB/SED

Figure 4.1   A typical business letter layout

Technical Literature

Nowadays, computer systems are an integral part of the accountant's working environment. As a result, many people must be able to use and interpret technical literature.

At all levels of use, technical literature must be clear and concise in the information it imparts. One can imagine what disasters would occur if information about a high voltage circuit was not made clear!

Technical literature transfers information from one source to another, provides new information, and is produced in a wide variety of forms.

Educational — this can be either in textbook format, or as articles written in newspapers and journals. It is written to make people aware of what is available and what can be done, and to inform them of the latest changes of thinking in any particular field of technology.

Instructional — the sales leaflet conveys a certain limited amount of instructional detail, such as uses, limitations, and a list of other details in compact form. Such things as equipment manuals for machinery explain to the operator how to set up and carry out operating drills. Other such items are emergency procedure tests and adjustments.

Within a company, and apart from high quality printed manuals and brochures, technical literature can take the form of memos or letters. These might identify the need for change, or suggest updating, or even the thoughts and aspirations of a genius who may well have re-designed a piece of equipment to be more cost effective.

Jargon is rife in the technical world. One set of jargon used in one factory or engineering research and development laboratory can be totally different from that in a similar factory. It has been known for the research and development engineers to totally mystify the manufacturing department by the use of jargon, resulting in a rather expensive time-wasting episode. In case of doubt, give definitions: 'in this study "robot" means . . .'.

Another problem that can arise in technical writing is the use of abbreviations. Only abbreviations known to everyone concerned should be used. If not, an appendix should accompany the document, laying out the abbreviations and their meanings.

Non-specific technical terms are another danger. Generalisation is dangerous in the technological world. Only specific terms should be used—one should never gamble on the 'he will know what I mean' attitude.

Poor English is another barrier. Unfortunately for the technical author, the old adage 'if it sounds right then it is right' does not necessarily follow in the technical world. All that is written must be clear and concise; there is no room for double meanings.

Technical literature demands technical excellence, which can only be gained by

- Diligent research
- Simple, concise, clear and accurate writing of facts, backed by excellent diagrammatic explanation
- Thorough checking by experts
- Trial on a target population.

Report Writing

Readability is the key to successful writing. A report must be interesting and easy to read if it is to have any impact. Readability can be achieved if a few simple rules are obeyed.

Report writers must start on a high point of interest. The title must catch the reader's attention much the same as a headline does in a newspaper.

Other points of interest must be introduced approximately every 500 words. This will of course depend upon the text, but in report writing 500 words gives plenty of time for the previous point to sink in.

In general, statistics should be used sparingly in the text, mathematical formulae should be avoided. The latter can always be covered in an appendix. The report must finish on a high point which makes the reader feel he has read a well-constructed and succinct document.

The need to consider the reader's interest in every paragraph is vital if you are to get the message across.

People reading a report may perhaps be trained in receiving, reading and understanding reports, but on the other hand they may not. The reader should not be expected to climb up to a high literary level: he won't, so don't attempt to make him.

Deciding on the length of the written work is important: if it is too short it may fail to get the complete message across; too long and it may lose your reader. Finding a balance is not easy. If you say the same thing more than once, ask yourself, 'Will the reader feel insulted by this repetition?' You can always say it in different words, but better still is to repeat it by reference: 'as shown above, the market for X is the fastest growing, but it needs further analysis'. One method that can be used is to write the piece, then try to reduce every paragraph by at least one sentence. Good editing is important. With practice the editing becomes less a process of mutilation and more a process of amendment.

Choosing the most appropriate format often depends on who the report is for. Some individuals like to receive correspondence and reports in a certain form. If so, use that form. If there is a choice, think about the people concerned—how long will they have to read it, and how involved and interested in the subject are they?

Style comes with experience. Let it happen naturally. Any attempt to develop a style artificially will lead to an unnatural flow.

No report should be written without a clearly defined objective. There are four principal reasons for writing reports but each report, regardless of the type, will have its own specific objective. If this is not clear to the writer then there is little hope of the report being effective.

The principal reasons for writing reports are:

- To obtain agreement to a course of action—persuasive
- To explain specific events—explanatory
- As a basis for discussion—discussive
- To inform—informative.

The reason for writing the report will determine the methods used. The objectives to be achieved will determine the exact form and the content used. Before starting work on a report the writer should ask himself the following three questions:

a) Why am *I* writing this report?

b) Which *type* of report should it be?

c) What are the *specific* objectives I hope to achieve?

There are a number of basic rules which should be followed for all types of reports. These are:

Brevity — If only a dozen words are needed do not write two hundred. Thin reports are attractive, easy to handle, cheap to produce, easy to change and usually much more readable. Nobody complains of the report being too short, provided it says something positive, and says it clearly.

Simplicity — A report is a means of communication, not the means to prove technical knowledge or demonstrate command of a large vocabulary. Only words that everyone will be able to read and understand should be used.

Purpose — Remember why the report is being written. It is all too easy to get lost in the process of writing. We all review our own writing as writers not as readers and consequently we often hide the message among too many words.

Beginning — Have a meaningful beginning that explains the reason for the report and introduces the reader to the subject. If the reader is aware of the report and the subject he can always skip the beginning.

Headings — These often act as signposts. They help the reader who may want to refer to the conclusions or recommendations subsequently.

Ending — Always end by summarising how the report has achieved its objectives. It is not necessary to actually write 'the end' but the reader should be quite clear that he has reached the end. (Remember the story of the preacher and the late arrival, who asked at the church door if the preacher had finished his sermon: the answer was, 'He's finished, but he won't stop'.)

Content — Make sure that the main content of the report is readable with points of interest well spaced throughout the report (eg every 500 words).

Jargon — Defined as 'the *unnecessary* use of technical terms', it should be vigorously avoided. If technical details are necessary keep them out of the body of the report.

Title — Give the report a short, meaningful title.

Author — Always name the writer or writers, and their status or function; a report should never be anonymous.

Date — Always date the report.

These basic rules should always be applied. All too often they are ignored and the results litter the files of any organisation.

Each of the four main types of reports—persuasive, explanatory, discussive and informative—have their own structure. For detailed information on how to write each kind of report more effectively there is a book entitled *Report Writing in Business*, also published by Kogan Page in association with the Chartered Institute of Management Accountants.

Chapter Five

The Spoken Word

To use the spoken word successfully we have to appreciate the way in which the spoken word is received and interpreted. There is a considerable difference between hearing and listening, and we need to understand this if we wish to communicate effectively.

The receiver must first hear the sounds uttered. These signals will be passed to the brain where they are sorted out. The brain filters out unwanted sounds, such as brackground noise. The filtering process continues until the brain identifies and interprets just one sound on which it decides to concentrate. This concentration on the sounds received is the act of listening.

Good listening requires a tremendous effort. However, it is very important since it assists the understanding of the message that is being transmitted.

Listening can avoid the need for time-wasting repetition. In order to listen one must concentrate on the message being received so that it can be fully understood. Understanding is a key element in successful listening. If we fail to understand a message it could be because it was badly constructed and transmitted, or because we did not listen carefully. If we do not listen carefully our brain is unable to decode the signals properly.

In the process of decoding the brain asks itself if what it is hearing is logical and whether it makes sense. If the answer is yes, it does make sense, then it moves on to the next stage of understanding. The brain begins to analyse all that is heard and to interpret the meaning.

It helps if the message is transmitted in the code (language) the brain has been trained to decode. If not, we can still hear the sounds, but there is no basis for understanding.

For understanding to take place, the transmitter must encode his message into a logical and sensible form in the right code (language), and then transmit it in a logical and sensible form. Even though the transmitter has made great efforts to ensure that in all cases he has been logical and sensible, understanding is totally dependent upon the receiver.

There are many potential distractions which can affect the way we listen. Visual distractions can be particularly disconcerting. At one seminar the presenter noticed that few of his audience were listening, but were concentrating on something different. He turned round to see the window cleaner working on the window and peering through a gap in the curtains.

Other concerns in our mind will affect our listening. The brain is geared to respond first to signals which affect our safety, survival signals. The need to catch a train will distract someone attending a meeting. He or she will keep checking their watch and working out how much time is left and so will not be listening.

Mood, too, can affect the will to listen. Someone in an aggressive mood will not listen as well as someone in a more peaceful mood, unless, of course, what he is hearing is adding fuel to the fire he is about to light.

If people are waiting to say something they are not listening except for a suitable opportunity to interrupt.

Attitude has a natural lead on to status. There are many people in relatively high office who consider it a chore to listen to those below them. Likewise, there are many who consider it a burden to listen to their superiors.

Vocabulary can also present difficulties to good listening. Long words are not easy to listen to or interpret. When we hear someone using long, seldom-used words, our understanding begins to fail. Suddenly the words no longer make sense or appear logical. The will to listen is impaired by the brain being in chaos as it tries to relate the words to a known situation or context.

Accents can have a similar effect, especially when they are combined with dialect. Unfamiliarity with such tones and strange words can again confuse the brain, provoking the eventual response, 'What on earth is he or she saying?'

It would be a dull world if everyone spoke in the same way, but we should all try to make sure that our diction is clear, short and simple.

We can hear without listening. In fact the only way to prevent ourselves from hearing is to take the deliberate step of blocking out sounds, either physically with earplugs, or mentally. The old saying puts it well: 'There's none so deaf as those who don't want to hear.'

A positive decision is taken to listen. All the time the brain is constantly questioning 'Do I' or 'Don't I' wish to continue listening? So long as the message content remains relevant concentration will remain. But if the level of relevance begins to subside, then concentration will lapse.

There are several factors which might cause our concentration to lapse:
- The language in which the message is coded
- The relevance of the message
- The conditions in which we receive it
- The vocabulary used
- Our attitude, mood and status.

When constructing a message to be transmitted by the spoken word, it is important to give careful thought to the above factors, and to make the task of listening as easy as possible for the intended recipient. This means ensuring that the message is clear, because it is simple, brief, and carries an appropriate emphasis.

Meetings

Meetings are an important part of the accountant's job. They are a crucial requirement for effective communication. Whether the purpose of the meeting is to take decisions or to pass information, it is equally important for the communication that takes place to be successful.

The first step is to ensure that everyone attending the meeting knows exactly why the meeting is being held, what it is hoped will be achieved, and what their own role in the meeting is to be.

The success of meetings depends largely on the chairperson (whom I shall call chairman from now on with no sexist implications), who can ensure effective communication by conducting the meeting properly. The job of the chairman is to see that the objectives of the meeting are achieved, by:

- Guiding
- Controlling
- Concentrating
- Clarifying
- Summarising.

The chairman has one objective, and only one—

TO SEE THAT THE OBJECTIVES
OF THE MEETING ARE MET.

So if the objectives have not been properly defined, there is no way the chairman can do his job. The chairman must make sure the agenda is followed (this is his controlling role) by doing three things. He must,

a) Stop people talking for too long
b) Draw out the more nervous people
c) Keep everyone to the point.

This kind of control is best achieved by personality and expertise rather than authority based on rank. Some gentle humour helps a chairman in this task, provided it is not at anybody's expense.

The chairman should help people to concentrate on what they are saying by using, for example, the 'Do you mean . . . ?' technique. This is a simple question which allows the chairman to focus on the nub of what the person is saying and allows the person to confirm the chairman's succinct appraisal.

It is also the chairman's job to make sure that everyone at the meeting understands what is being said. He should stop people and ask them to explain technical terms. He must ask questions when he thinks explanation is needed, and if necessary he should go round the table and ask if everyone has understood.

Finally the chairman must summarise and make sure that

- All points of action are agreed and the person and time for completion are accepted
- All decisions are fully understood and agreed.

This summary, if done properly, will provide a schedule of points to be followed up after the meeting.

Follow-up to meetings

The chairman is responsible for the follow-up to the meeting. He may delegate the work, but he must make sure it is done. The follow-up normally consists of two elements:

a) The minutes
b) Checking on action and decisions.

Minutes

Formal minutes are intended to produce a minute-by-minute record of what goes on at the meeting. Early minute books actually had the times printed down the side of the page.

Minutes, however recorded, should provide the following information:

1. Attendances
2. The agenda
3. The main points discussed
4. The points for action and the name of the person responsible for taking action
5. The decisions taken
6. The decisions deferred and the date to which they were deferred
7. The time the meeting finished.

The chairman can considerably aid his secretary by going through these main headings in his summary of the meeting.

Checking on action

Of course, to simply list points for action does not mean they will necessarily be carried out—it is up to the chairman to check. This has three very important effects:

1. The person concerned realises that his action is being observed and is more keen to get on with it
2. Any problems he has in taking action can be discussed and resolved
3. It clearly indicates that the chairman takes the meeting seriously and this rubs off on other people.

If at the end of the meeting everyone in attendance feels that the objectives have been achieved and the meeting was a necessary component in achieving them, then the meeting has been a success. This, in reality, is the only true measure of the success of meetings. There are far too many meetings that end with one or more people wondering why the meeting was called in the first place.

The success of meetings also depends upon the individuals attending the meeting. Each person should carefully consider what they want to achieve and what they want to say. At a recent meeting, a person who rarely said anything was asked why he bothered attending. His answer is worth repeating.

> 'I only speak when I have something to say and
> I only learn when I listen.'

There are a number of techniques available to anyone attending meetings, each concerned with what is done and said, and when it is done or said.

Knowing when to make a contribution is essential, and depends to some extent on what is being contributed. It has been said that there are only four things to do at a meeting:

a) Ask a question
b) Answer a question
c) Make a suggestion (we ought to launch it later, not earlier)
d) Pass an opinion (their competitive position is weaker than it was).

Asking questions
Questions should be asked in such a way as to provide answers which either clarify or inform. They should not be asked to prove that the other person is unable to answer, or simply to make a contribution. A good chairman can easily turn such a question against the questioner. If clarification or more information is needed, it may help to preface the question with 'I'm not clear about X . . . ' or 'Can we have some more information on Y . . . ?'

Answering questions
An answer should never be given unless it is known to be correct. If

the answer is not known, say so, and say it will be found. If it is a crucial point in the discussion, apologise and ask the chairman if the point can be deferred until the next meeting.

Making suggestions

It is unfortunate but true that many people attending meetings avoid making suggestions because of the possibility that they will be ridiculed by other people at the meeting. The chairman can help here by commenting that it is a good or useful suggestion and by making sure it is properly discussed. Only very experienced and very confident people should make 'off the cuff' suggestions.

Passing opinions

This is a fairly safe thing to do because everyone has an opinion. However, to have the greatest impact wait until the chairman invites a comment. This implies that he values the views expressed. But do not wait too long for he may not ask for an opinion.

Timing

Timing is another important meeting technique. It is normally preferable to time contributions so that other people's views can be evaluated before influencing them. However, if it is necessary to get a particular decision taken, then it is perhaps better to speak first so that other people are influenced before they have committed themselves. This can often be arranged with the chairman before the meeting and implies that the chairman thinks the comments should be heard which is always an advantage.

If not directly involved or concerned with a particular topic, leave comments until the end of the discussion so that the pros and cons can be weighed up. If it is played right the unbiased views will be respected.

'Speech is silver, but silence is golden', (Thomas Carlyle). Silence is an excellent technique if used properly. It can mean:

- I disagree
- I do not care

- I am thinking)   ie I have not made
- I am waiting   )   up my mind
- I agree.

Silence used with movements and gestures, such as shaking of the head, raised eyebrows, frown, etc, all help to indicate what is being thought. Make sure, however, that silence is not misinterpreted. It takes skill and experience to use silence effectively but when the skill has been acquired, it becomes an excellent servant.

Lobbying

Lobbying is always associated with politics, whether within a company or in parliament, but it can be a very effective way of achieving one's objectives in meetings. All meetings involve some form of politics—the more serious the meeting the more politics are involved. It becomes important to know where everyone stands on the various points to be discussed.

Lobbying is an activity which must be carried out with care. Being too open can provide 'the other side' with the information they need. Most meetings take place without this cut and thrust which can become vicious, but unfortunately, as one gets nearer the top of a company, it can become more and more important until it can eventually obscure the real objectives of a meeting.

Friendly lobbying for support for suggestions and opinions is perfectly good, but be open about it and discuss your ideas with everyone due to attend so that there is no suggestion of connivance to overcome real objections.

Using the Telephone

The telephone is an instant way of communication that is simple and relatively cheap to use. However, people have a tendency to use it as a stop-gap in the everyday need to communicate, which can often cause confusion and misrepresentation. The effectiveness of the telephone as a means of communication is solely dependent upon the user.

As a communications medium for the spoken word it creates several problems. The caller tends to assume that the person being called is in the same position, with all the facts to hand for example, whereas it is more than likely that only the caller himself has all the relevant papers in front of him.

Furthermore, the messages that are communicated by telephone cannot be filed word for word as letters can. Only a summarised version conforming to the receiver's or the transmitter's interpretation will be retained.

The essence of good telephone use can be summed up as follows:

- Before making the call prepare the message (the objective) carefully
- Smile and dial
- Identify yourself by name and, if necessary, by appointment and the organisation you represent, when the telephone is answered
- Identify the person with whom you wish to speak, by name or their appointment
- Deliver your message
- Take any notes necessary during the call
- Confirm that the message has been received and understood
- End the call
- Update your files
- Update any staff who need to know of changes brought about by the call
- Carry out any other form of follow-up.

Whether receiving or originating telephone calls, it is important to always be polite, and to be as brief and as helpful as possible. Always thank the person you are speaking to, and if you are the wrong person answering, say so.

Always use a telephone record pad wherever possible—it is there as a written reminder and is essential in today's all-action world.

Presentation Techniques

The effectiveness and efficiency of all presentations will largely depend upon the ability of the presenter. The key to successful presentation is the imaginative and commonsense application of three principles and two techniques.

The principles of presentation:
a) Promotion and maintenance of the desire to listen
b) Preparation and planning
c) Confirmation that the presentation has been assimilated.

The techniques of presentation:
a) The question technique
b) The selection and use of instructional aids.

These principles and techniques are not to be treated separately or in isolation. They are closely interrelated and need to be applied in combination according to circumstances.

Promotion and maintenance of the desire to listen
An audience cannot be forced to listen. People only listen when they are willing to listen, and they understand the reason and purpose behind the presentation. Their attention can be quickly lost by bungling.

An audience needs to be encouraged, led, stimulated into wanting to listen and into continuing to listen throughout the presentation. A presentation must, therefore, be planned with this in mind.

It is largely a matter of purposefully promoting and maintaining interest, which in turn secures the willing co-operation of the audience.

Preparation and planning

All presentations require thorough, step-by-step preparation, taking into consideration all the relevant factors. Careful and systematic planning must follow so that the material is presented logically and progressively in the best possible way to enable the audience to understand the message.

For every section of the presentation, the presenter requires a clear plan that will show:

a) What he expects the audience to do as a result of the presentation
b) What he must get over
c) How he is going to do it
d) What aids and administrative arrangements he needs to make.

The plan must also take into account the conditions under which the presentation will take place.

Confirmation that the presentation has been assimilated

The presenter has the responsibility to make sure that his presentation is being understood. Each stage of the presentation must lead the audience towards understanding the message. At the end of a presentation, both the presenter and his audience need to know whether they have succeeded; the presenter in presenting, and the audience in listening and understanding.

However, presentation skills cannot be gained solely from reading a book, no matter how helpful the information that is provided may be. They are gained by doing presentations. Nevertheless, it is possible to provide a number of guidelines to potential presenters.

Perhaps one of the key points is to try not to say too much. Most presenters try to pack far too much into their presentations. They then speak too quickly, in a constant monotone, because they are more interested in getting it all said instead of persuading their audience to listen. To avoid putting too much into a presentation the following formula can be followed:

1. A written speech should contain no more than 60 words for every minute of speaking time.
2. Every presentation should be divided into three sections with a time limit on each:
    a) Introduction (10%)
    b) Main body (70%)
    c) Summary (20%).
3. Spend no more than 5 minutes on each main point in the body of the presentation.

Following this formula, a plan for a 30 minute presentation will look something like this:

	Time in minutes	Words in speech
Introduction	3	180
Main body — Point 1	5	300
2	5	300
3	5	300
4	5	300
Summary and conclusion	7	420
	30	1800

This plan indicates that four main points can be made successfully and that the written version of the speech should not exceed 1800 words.

The second key point is to make the presentation as natural as possible. The best way of achieving this is to reduce the written words into a series of notes and to use these as the basis for the speech. This creates a more personal style than reading a speech out verbatim. Notes can be prepared in various ways using paper or small cards. A suggested approach is to prepare one page for each of the elements in the plan, ie

> Introduction
> Point 1
>   2
>   3
>   4
> Summary and conclusion

At the top of the page will be the headline followed by a series of sub-headings, each of which is supported by key words and phrases.

The third key point in successful presenting is the choice of words and phrases. Long words and phrases should always be avoided: the wording should be short, brief and punchy.

The fourth main point can be summarised in two words—media variety. A presentation that has a talk, visual aids and perhaps a film would be better than one relying only on the spoken word. The aim is to get the audience to participate with more than one sense and in a variety of ways. Another way of achieving this is to ask the audience for a show of hands, or to ask them to fill in a short questionnaire. It demonstrates that you, the presenter, care about the audience, and it is hoped that they will go away in a good frame of mind, with the intended message.

The appearance of the presenter is very important when making presentations. Presenters should be smartly dressed appropriate to the occasion and the environment. If they are not, then their appearance will be a distraction to the audience. The presenter has a big enough problem in getting and keeping the audience's attention, without creating his own distractions!

Delivery is mainly a matter of practice. Such matters as stance, voice and style will, of course, depend very much on the individual.

Perhaps the only advice that can be given here is to be as natural as possible.

Using the spoken word as a means of communication offers many opportunities, but it also carries threats for the unprepared presenter. Careful planning and preparation, rehearsal and practice are the only way to achieve success.

Chapter Six

Visual Media

Visual signals have always been an important part of the communication process. The sense of sight is not only highly sophisticated, it is also capable of dealing with a very wide range of signals received in a variety of ways and at high speed. It is not accidental that road signs are simple visual symbols. The message has to be received and understood by the brain very fast indeed.

Many visual symbols are used to overcome language problems. Gestures and sign language, facial expressions and body movements are all part of the visual communication process.

Visual communication can be used to complement both the written and the spoken word. Modern communication devices allow the construction of very effective messages for all forms of communication. The main forms of visual signals are:

- Pictures, both still and moving
- Cartoons and illustrations
- Diagrams
- Charts and graphs
- Signs.

Such images can be presented in a wide variety of forms, such as:

- Printed
- Slides
- Films
- Video
- Models, static and working.

Pictures

Pictures should be carefully selected to emphasise the point of the message for which they are used. Both black and white, and colour can be used depending upon the circumstances. Pictures should be clear, simple and add impact to the message.

Cartoons and Illustrations

There are occasions when pictures are not available or cannot easily be produced, in which case artists' cartoons and illustrations can be used with great effect. They should, of course, be produced by professionals, unless talented amateurs are available.

Diagrams

Diagrams such as flowcharts, networks, process flow diagrams, room plans, factory layouts, etc, can all have a major part to play in effective communication. Once again they should be produced with great care, to scale, and be an accurate representation of the function or activity being depicted.

Charts and Graphs

Charts and graphs can now be produced with ease and to a very high quality using computers. Once again, they should be clear, simple and bring impact to the message being communicated.

Graphs are particularly relevant in the world of accounting which is so concerned with numerical data.

Numbers can often be presented most effectively using graphics. The idea of graphs is quite simple. Most numerical data is presented in comparison with another factor, which might be time or other data. By using the two dimensions of vertical and horizontal, information can be presented in a variety of ways.

The aim of a graph is a show relationships easily and directly without the need for reading the detailed figures. These should, of course, be available if needed.

The table shown in Figure 6.1 can be represented effectively as a graph (see Figure 6.2).

Leisurefare Ltd — Sales (£)

	Radios	Hi-Fi	Records	Tapes	Total
1982	31,250	18,000	24,000	8,925	82,185
1983	36,300	24,850	29,050	12,115	102,315
1984	34,750	32,925	38,875	21,915	128,465
1985	32,800	36,876	44,925	30,825	145,425
1986	35,000	40,925	46,875	40,215	163,015

Figure 6.1   Information represented in the form of a table

In the same way as graphs, bar charts have a vertical and a horizontal axis, but then use solid blocks or bars to show relationships. The bars may be placed either horizontally or vertically. The majority of bar charts use the vertical axis for showing value and the horizontal axis for time or comparable units. There are two ways that the data in Figure 6.1 can be presented, each having a different impact. Figure 6.3 shows the sales of each product in relation to the others, while Figure 6.4 shows the proportion of the total attributable to each product: Figure 6.4 should be used if the emphasis is on total sales; Figure 6.3 if the emphasis is on product sales.

The horizontal approach is used mainly for progress charts which record the planned and actual progress of activities against time, as shown in Figure 6.5.

Only primary colours—red, blue, green and black—should be used on graphs and charts; other colours are either too pale or too similar.

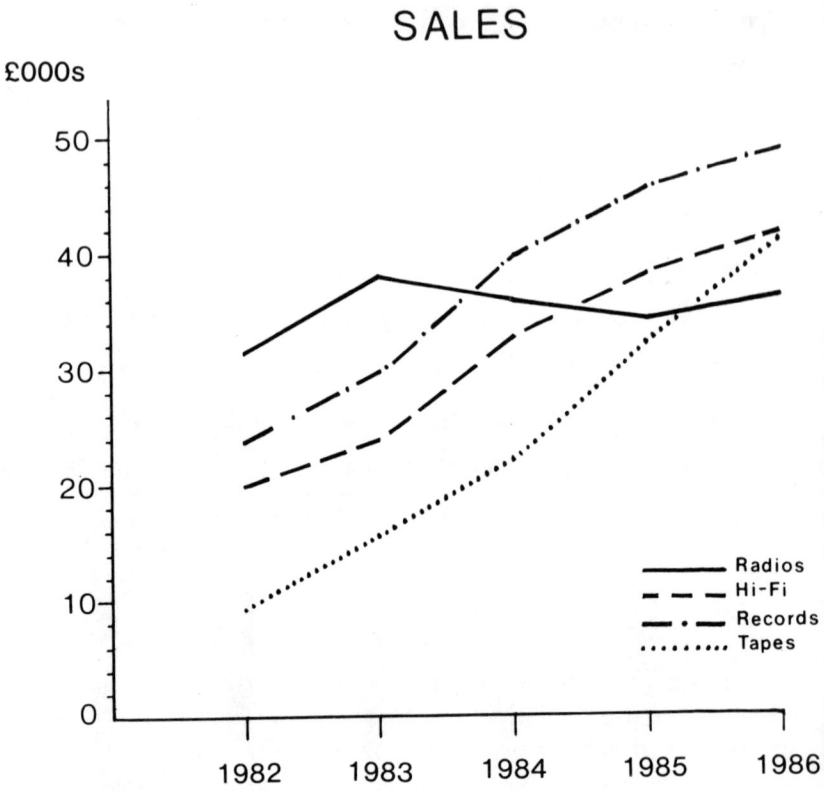

Figure 6.2   Information represented in the form of a graph

For black and white charts and graphs only four representations should be used:

   a) Solid black lines and blocks
   b) Dotted lines and blocks
   c) Broken lines and striped blocks
   d) Dash and dot lines, grey or empty blocks.

This enables printed material to be photocopied to good effect.

SALES

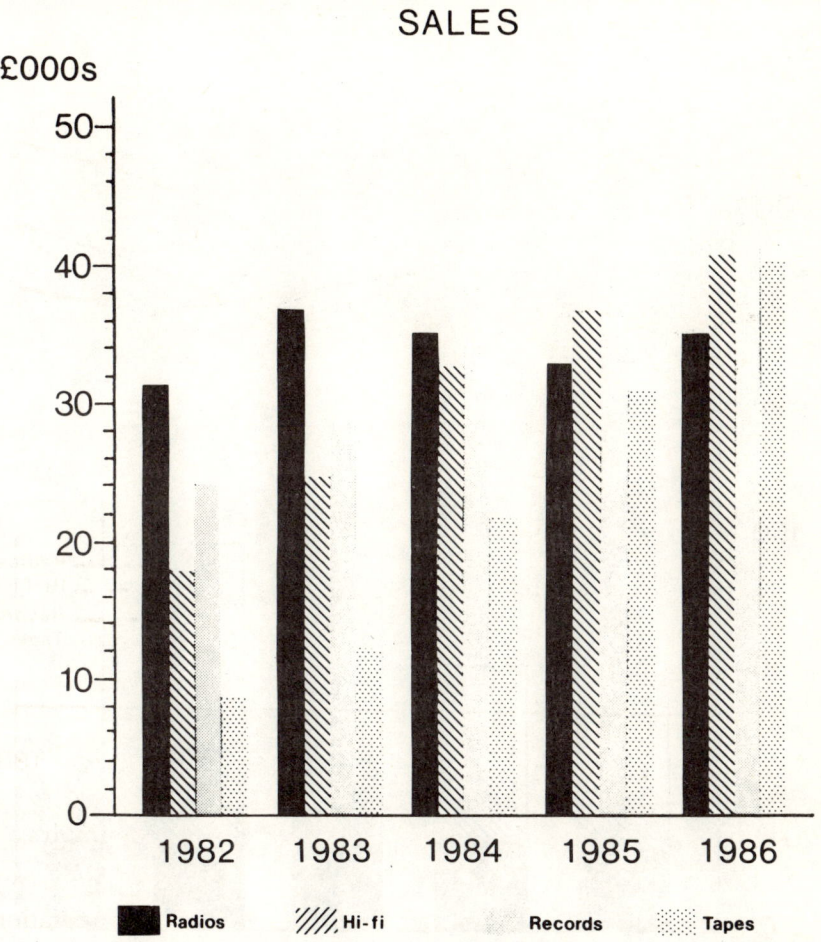

Figure 6.3   Information represented in the form of a bar chart

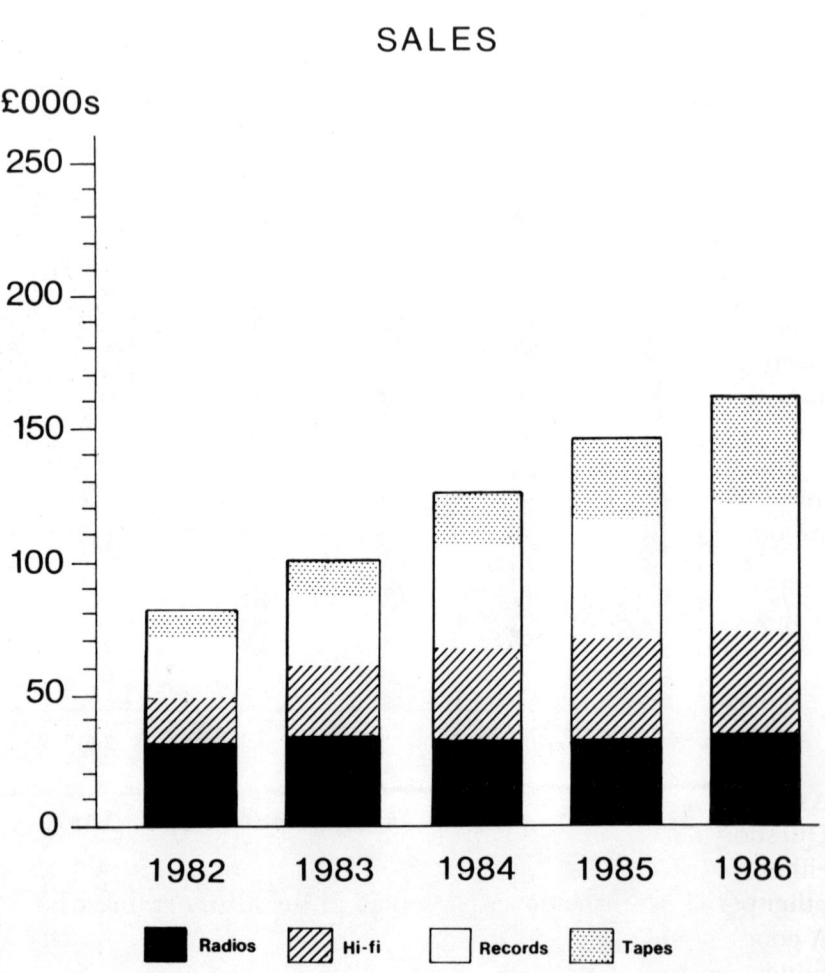

Figure 6.4 Information represented in the form of a block chart

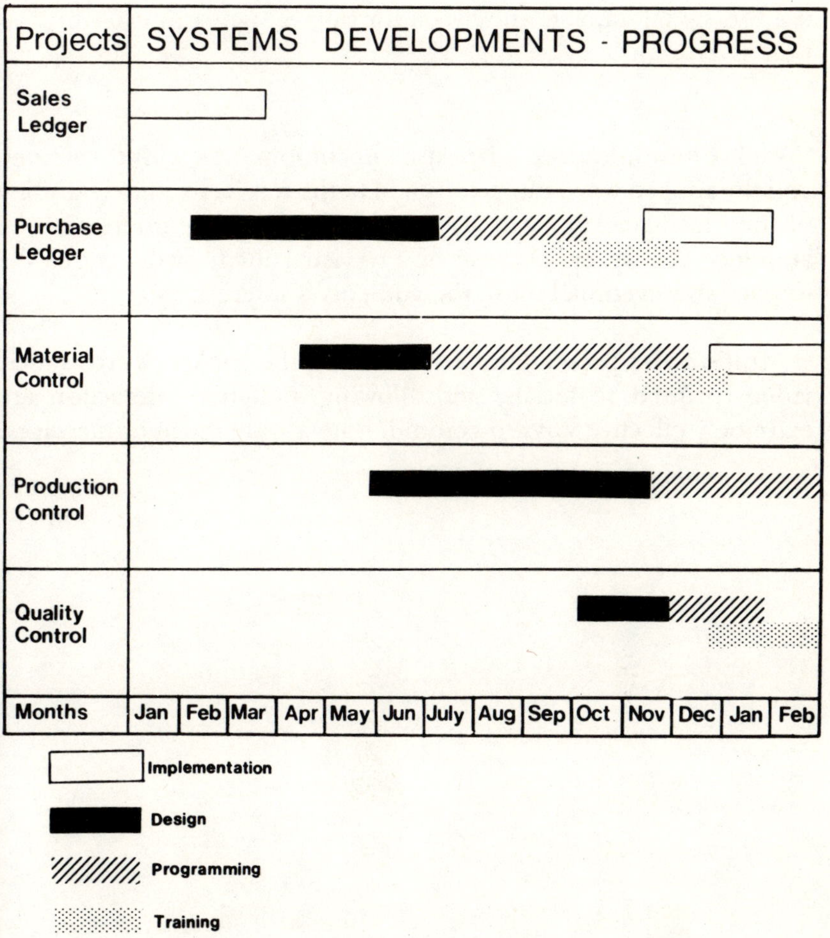

Figure 6.5 Information represented in the form of a progress chart

Signs

Signs are used in all kinds of situations, particularly for names and directions. Colours are also a key element in signs with red being used to signal danger, and green for safety. Signs can use words as well as symbols.

Visual communications when used in combination with the written and the spoken word can greatly add to the receiver's understanding of the message. They can also attract and keep the interest of the audience. However, overuse of any visual media will reduce the impact and eventually lose the audience's interest.

Multi-media presentations, combining the spoken word, slides, video, printed materials, and allowing audience interaction are extremely effective ways to communicate a wide range of messages.

Chapter Seven

Barriers to Communication

There are eight main barriers which need to be overcome if communication is to be effective. These are:

- Language
- Vocabulary
- Class
- Attitude
- Position
- Personality and Character
- Mood
- Knowledge of Subject.

Language

It is obvious that if we do not speak the same language we are going to fail to communicate effectively. In some circumstances gestures (sign language) can achieve limited success. If we are transmitting information we should take care to see that our audience do at least use the same language. A message will be far more effective if it is sent in the language used by the recipient; it should not be assumed that he will take the trouble to translate something he cannot understand.

Vocabulary

'The predilection to perpetrate incomprehensible formulations of loquacious literary publications should be strenuously discouraged by those responsible for the dissemination of information'—or, the use of big words should be avoided when communicating.

Whenever we prepare a message of any kind we should remember that the vocabulary of most people is very limited. Proving that yours is not does little to assist the communication process. There is no greater compliment for a speaker or writer than to be told that what he has written or said is understandable and logical. This does not mean that only the reader or listener found it easy to read or listen, but that he also understood the words.

Class

It may be surprising that this measure of social status is included, but it is often a fundamental barrier to effective communication. For it is not only the language and the words used that are important, but also the way we use them, and this is mainly determined by our social background and environment. There are many advertisements asking for persons who are able 'to communicate with all levels of management'. It requires considerable tact and understanding to do this effectively.

Attitude

A receiver's attitude can be set by the method of approach employed by the transmitter. Even the facial expressions of a transmitter can have an effect upon the receiver. Words can be used to convey displeasure or delight. So the way we address a receiver should be adapted to the content of the message.

Stance, the way we stand or sit when transmitting, can trigger 'guard' or 'relax' mechanisms in a receiver. It requires a very clever person to deliver a message of rebuke without disturbing the attitude of a receiver. There are few people who can deliver such messages with poise, charm and grace, but nevertheless it is possible.

Position

Perhaps one of the most difficult communication problems with people stems from the direction of the communication. There is no doubt that people communicate differently with their bosses, their staff and their colleagues, not only in the way they transmit their messages, but also in the attention which they give them.

Personality and Character

No matter how hard we try there are some people with whom we just cannot reach an understanding. We are all individuals with our own personalities and characters, which help determine how we are treated by other people. Some characteristics impinge directly on our ability to communicate effectively.

It is not easy to change personalities but attitudes can be altered. We should start by examining our own attitudes and personality, and gauge the effect we have on other people. We must find ways of minimising the adverse impact upon communications of things in our make-up we cannot change. It is rightly said that we are unaware of our impact on others until we see ourselves on video, with sound, and realise how many irritating habits we have.

Mood

The old saying, 'There's a time and place for everything' is particularly true of communication. Said at the wrong time and in the wrong place, the simplest of words can cause chaos. Testing the mood is like testing the water before jumping into the pool. A good communicator tests the mood and responds to it. Moods may be created by an individual or by groups. Responding to both types of mood is important if we are to communicate effectively. A person who cannot judge the atmosphere will fail to choose the right moment to pass on this message, and in so doing will fail to communicate.

Knowledge of Subject

It is important, of course, to have a knowledge of the subject you need to communicate on, but this can also be a danger. One thing that should be established is whether the receiver's knowledge is greater than that of the transmitter, or vice versa. To show appreciation for another's knowledge helps break down the communication barriers.

It is fair to suggest that the 'people problems' in communication are the major ones. The common suggestion that faulty communications can be cured by better devices is usually untrue. They can certainly be made faster and spread further, but unless the basic 'people problems' are overcome, modern technology will interfere rather than assist in our attempts to communicate.

The Transmitter

The transmitter must also identify within himself exactly the same problems as the receiver. If the transmitter does not speak the same language as the receiver, then it can be regarded as his duty to translate the message into the receiver's tongue before he transmits it.

Vocabulary also causes problems and can irritate enough to affect the response of the receiver. If we know the receiver then we can pitch the vocabulary at the mutually agreed level, but if not, observe caution and keep it simple.

How does class affect the transmitter? The test we can do here is to recognise where we see ourselves in comparison to the receiver. At all costs, class should be removed from all communication wherever possible, if only for the sake of obeying the rules of good manners and respect for fellow human beings.

The tone of the communication can be set by the transmitter. A whole string of adjectives can be used to set an attitude: lethargic, laconic, aggressive, domineering, arrogant, and so on. The attitude set will be decided by the intentions of the message.

The position or status of the transmitter can have a very similar bearing on communication as that of attitude. The effect on the receiver is dependent upon which side of the scale he is on, ie above or below the transmitter. There are few people who are aggressive to those above them without first finding just cause, but obviously it is easy to be aggressive downwards. Thus, there is a direct relationship between attitude and position.

Personality and character can be adapted to suit the needs of the receiver, dependent upon the receiver's knowledge of the transmitter. It is a question of body chemistry. A good relationship usually ensures good communication. A poor relationship can have the opposite result. Adaptability to the mind of the intended receiver is a difficult skill to master and use correctly, but many people do master it.

The mood of the transmitter can upset or enhance that of the receiver. Communication can be set on a simple scale: a good mood results in good communication; a bad mood, in bad communication. Remember mood is a two-way thing—and both parties can, accidentally or otherwise, reinforce it or defuse it.

A good transmitter will put himself in the place of the receiver. A good receiver will put himself in the place of the transmitter. The ability to do this will increase the measure of understanding of each party.

Communication Needs

Our individual communication needs, both as transmitters and receivers, vary considerably. They depend upon the job we do, the size of the organisation, the geographical spread of the company, the way activities are organised and the style of management. Each individual will have to assess his own needs and apply what he learns accordingly.

It was stated earlier that listening was a vital part of communication. Although listening is not a natural ability, it can be developed by people being prepared to use their ears more than their mouth.

Chapter Eight

Effective Communication

Effective communication takes place when the transmitter constructs and delivers a message in such a way that the receiver gets and understands the message and responds in exactly the way the transmitter intended.

This means that the transmitter must know exactly what he or she is trying to achieve, and must select the best possible way of forming and delivering the message so that his objective is reached.

The golden rules for success are,

- Simplicity
- Brevity
- Directness
- Impact.

When coupled with imagination, they will enable effective communication to take place. Complicated ideas, long sentences, long words and complex visual signals only get in the way.

For the accountant the problem of communicating effectively is made more difficult because of the extensive use of jargon and his need to communicate large amounts of numerical information. However, these problems can be overcome; the accountant who succeeds in simplifying and clarifying his message will find that the impact he has on management decision-making will grow and be more widely recognised.

This book has examined the principles of good communication. It has discussed communicating via the written word, the spoken word and via visual signals. In all of these great emphasis has been placed on the importance of the way the message is received. However, it is all too easy to blame the receiver for failing to understand. In fact, if a particular attempt at communication fails, it *is* solely the fault of the transmitter.

Unless this is accepted then no one can begin to develop communication skills. Far too many accountants blame receivers for failing to understand but, when one looks at the way many accountants try to construct and deliver their messages, it is not surprising that their audience fails to understand.

Simply because we can read, write, speak and hear does not mean we can necessarily communicate. Before we can do that, we have to learn how to transmit and receive messages. We have to practise what we have learnt and we have to continually strive to get better.

Communication is about transferring ideas and information between people. It is the key to harmonious relationships, both socially and at work. Unless we gain the skill to communicate effectively, we will fail to be effective in all aspects of our lives. To be considered by one's peers to be a good communicator is perhaps one of the highest accolades we can receive.

It is interesting to note that good communicators stand out, because there are so few of them. The aim of this book has been to help you become a good communicator. The rest is up to you to practise and improve. And please remember if people do not understand you, it is your fault, not theirs.

Index

abbreviations, use of, 39
accents, and dialects, 47
accountants, role as com-
    municator, 11–13
action
    as communication stage, 15, 20–
    21
    following meetings, 50
agenda, 48–9, 50
appearance of presenter, 58
attitude, 46
    as communication barrier, 32,
    70, 72
audience, reader as, 31, 32–4
author, of reports, 42

bar charts, 63, 65
barriers to communication, 18,
    21
    attitude, 33, 70, 72
    class, 70, 72
    communication needs, 73
    knowledge of subject, 32, 71–2
    language, 12, 32, 69, 72
    mood, 33, 71, 73
    personality and character, 33,
    71, 73
    position, 32, 70–71, 72–3
    transmitter's problems, 72–3
    vocabulary, 32, 69–70, 72

beginning, of reports, 42
block charts, 63–4, 66
body language, 27, 29
brevity, 25, 34, 41, 75

cartoons, 62
chairman, of meetings, 48–50
character, 33
    as communication barrier, 71,
    73
charts, 62–7 .
clarity, 25, 34
class, as communication barrier,
    70, 72,
colour, in visual media, 62, 63–4
communication
    accountant's role, 11–13
    barriers, see barriers to com-
    munication
    effective, 75–6
    needs, 73
    principles of, 15–21
complaint writing/answering, 34–
    5
confirmation, presentation prin-
    ciple, 55, 56
content, of reports, 39–40, 41–2
control, of meetings, 48–9
correspondence, 11, 35–6, 37

date, of reports, 42
delivery, of presentation, 58–9
diagrams, 62
dialects, and accents, 47
directness, 75
discussions, face to face, 11
discussive reports, 11, 41, 42

editing, of reports, 40
educational technical literature,
    38
ending, of reports, 42
explanatory reports, 11, 41, 42

facial expression, 70
feedback, 15
filtering process, of sounds, 45
financial statements, 11
follow-up, of meetings, 49–50
formation, communication stage,
    15, 17–18

generalisations, use of, 39
gestures, 18, 27, 29, 53, 61, 69
grammar, 24
graphs, 62–4

headings, of reports, 42

illustrations, 62
impact, need for, 75
inflexion, use of, 24, 32
informative reports, 11, 41, 42
instructional aids, 55
instructional technical literature,
    38
instructions, written, 36
interpreting signals, 19–20
interviews, 11

jargon, 12, 75
    reports, 38–9, 42

knowledge of subjects, 32, 71–2

language
    as communication barrier, 12,
        32, 69, 72
    grammar, 24
    of messages, code, 46, 47
layout, of letters, 35–6, 37
layout rule, of numbers, 26
letter writing, 35–6, 37
listening, 45–8, 55, 73
lobbying, at meetings, 53

media variety, presentations, 58
meetings, 11
    chairman's role, 48–50
    contributions, 51–3
    follow-up, 49–50
    objectives, 48–9
memos, 36, 38
messages
    formation, 15, 17–18
    relevance, 47–8
    signals and, 23–9
minutes, 49–50
mood, 46
    as communication barrier, 33,
        71, 73
multi-media presentations, 23,
    68

non-specific technical terms, 39
numbers, 13, 18, 23, 25–6
    charts and graphs, 62–7

objectives
    of meetings, 48–9
    reports, 40–41
    writer's, 32
    see also purpose
opinions, passing, at meetings, 52
order rule, numbers, 25–6

paragraphs, formation of, 25
perception, communication stage,
    15, 19–20
persuasive reports, 11, 41, 42
pictures, 18, 23, 27, 61
planning, presentation principle,
    56
position, 46–7
    as communication barrier, 32, 70–
    71, 72–3
preparation, presentation princi-
    ple, 56
presentation techniques, spoken
    word, 55–9
presentations, formal/informal,
    11
presenter, appearance of, 58
progress charts, 63, 67
purpose
    communication stage, 15, 16–
    17
    of reports, 42
    see also objectives

questions
    asking/answering, 34–5
    at meetings, 51–2

readability, of reports, 39, 40
reader, as audience, 31, 32–4
receiver, 16–17

communication barriers, 32–3,
    69–72, 73
    listening, 45–8, 55, 73
    reading, 31, 32–4
receiving signals, 19–20
reception, communication stage,
    15, 19
recognising signals, 19–20
report writing, 11, 39–43
Report Writing in Business, 43

sentences, formation of, 24–5
sign language, 61, 69
signals, 19–20
    messages and, 23–9
    spoken word, 45–8
significance rule, of numbers, 25
signs, 61, 68
silence, meeting technique, 52–3
simplicity, 24, 33, 41, 75
sincerity, 33
situations, communication, 11
social class, as communication
    barrier, 70, 72
sounds, 20, 29, 45
spoken word
    listening, 45–8, 55, 73
    meetings, 48–53
    presentation techniques, 55–9
    telephone, 53–5
stance, of transmitter, 58, 70
statistics, in reports, 40
style, of reports, 40
subject
    knowledge of, 32, 71–2
    of written word, 31–2
suggestions, at meetings, 52
symbols, 18, 26–7, 61

tables, 26, 63
technical literature, 38–9
telephone, 11, 53–5
timing technique
    at meetings, 52–3
    for presentations, 57
title, of reports, 39, 42
transmission, communication
        stage, 15, 18–19
transmitter, 15–17
    accountant's role, 11–13
    communication barriers, 72–3
    effective communication, 75–6
    presenter, appearance of, 58

visual images, 20, 26–9

visual media, 61–8
vocabulary, 47
    as communication barrier, 32,
        69–70, 72

words, 18, 23–5
    in speech, 56–9
    spoken, *see* spoken word
    written, *see* written word
written word
    basic rules, 31–43
    instructions, 36
    letters, 35–6, 37
    reports, 39–43
    technical literature, 38–9